Feet and Puppies, Thieves and Guppies

What Are Irregular Plurals?

For my parents
—B.P.C.

Irregular Plurals:
Plural words
that are not
formed by the
usual pattern of
adding -s or -es

Feet and Puppies, Thieves and Guppies

What Are Irregular Plurals?

by Brian P. Cleary

illustrations by Brian Gable

M MILLBROOK PRESS / MINNEAPOLIS

Cats and hats and acrobats,
hamsters, squares, and squirrels—

SQUARE DANCE TONIGHT

because they all name more than one, these words are known as plurals.

Plural means there's two or more of something, like these dresses.

Shoes and shades and lemonades—
See how they end in S's?

Adding S or e-s to most nouns
will make them plural.

But you won't find two "foots" on any yardstick,

boy,

or girl!

9

You see, "foot" is irregular. The plural form is "feet."

TWO FEET

Many words that end in *y*
Will end in *i-e-s*

The singular is "buddy," and the plural form is "buddies."

This rule applies to lots of words, like **candies**, babies, studies, guppies, puppies, parties, pennies, jellies, bellies, berries,

mommies, daddies, flies, and paddies, ponies, skies, and cherries.

If an f-e ends your word,
then swap f for a V

16

in plural forms.

Take wives
and knives
and lives,

to name just three.

Often, when *f* ends the word, the plural makes this change:

the **f** turns into **v–e–s**, as in, "These loaves are strange."

LEAF→LEAVES LOAF→LOAVES
CALF→CALVES

HALF→HALVES

WOLF→WOLVES

THIEF→THIEVES

SELF→SELVES

Some words, when they end in O, need e-s when they're plural,

as in, "I see potatoes and tomatoes on that mural."

Sometimes plurals change the vowels, like tooth becoming teeth.

Like man to men,

or mouse to mice

or goose becoming geese.

others? Seems they had no rules
when the language folks devised 'em.

* Plurals *

Like child becoming children—
We just have to memorize 'em!

Certain nouns, when plural,
always stay the same throughout,

like deer and moose and bison,
sheep and salmon,
swine and trout.

I wrote this book so kids could keep it handy on their shelves

So what is an **irregular plural?**

Do you know?

We usually form plurals by adding s or es to the end of the word. We add es when the word ends in s, x, ch, or sh. Irregular plurals don't follow these rules. This chart will help you know when an irregular plural is called for—and how to form it.

Word ending	To form irregular plural	Example
-fe	Change f to v, then add -s	knife → knives
-f	Change f to v, then add -es	half → halves
-o	Add -es	tomato → tomatoes
-us	Change -us to -i	cactus → cacti
-is	Change -is to -es	analysis → analyses
-on	Change -on to -a	phenomenon → phenomena
Any ending	Change the vowel	foot → feet
Any ending	Change the word	person → people
Any ending	Singular/plural are the same	sheep, deer

Find activities, games, and more at
www.brianpcleary.com

ABOUT THE AUTHOR & ILLUSTRATOR

BRIAN P. CLEARY is the author of the best-selling Words Are CATegorical® series as well as the Math Is CATegorical®, Food Is CATegorical™, Adventures in Memory™, and Sounds Like Reading® series. He has also written Six Sheep Sip Thick Shakes: And Other Tricky Tongue Twisters, The Punctuation Station, and several other books. Mr. Cleary lives in Cleveland, Ohio.

BRIAN GABLE is the illustrator of many Words Are CATegorical® books and the Math Is CATegorical® series. Mr. Gable also works as a political cartoonist for the Globe and Mail newspaper in Toronto, Canada.

Text copyright © 2012 by Brian P. Cleary
Illustrations copyright © 2012 by Lerner Publishing Group, Inc.

Millbrook Press
A division of Lerner Publishing Group, Inc.
241 First Avenue North
Minneapolis, MN 55401 U.S.A.

Website address: www.lernerbooks.com

Main body text set in RandumTEMP 35/48.
Typeface provided by House Industries.

Library of Congress Cataloging-in-Publication Data

Cleary, Brian P., 1959—
    Feet and puppies, thieves and guppies : what are irregular plurals? / by Brian P. Cleary, illustrations by Brian Gable.
        p.   cm. — (Words Are CATegorical)
    ISBN: 978—0—7613—4918—1 (lib. bdg. : alk. paper)
    1. English language—Number—Juvenile literature. 2. English language—Noun—Juvenile literature.
I. Gable, Brian, 1949—, ill.   II. Title.
PE1216.C54 2012
428.1—dc23   2011022387

Manufactured in the United States of America
1 — DP — 12/31/11